ADVENTURES OF THE MINECRAFT TWINS

BOOK 1

MEET THE TOWER WIZARD

RICK REDSTONE

An Unofficial Minecraft Book

© Copyright 2022 - All rights reserved.

The contents of this book may not be reproduced, duplicated or transmitted without direct written permission from the author.

Under no circumstances will any legal responsibility or blame be held against the publisher for any reparation, damages, or monetary loss due to the information herein, either directly or indirectly.

Legal Notice:

This book is copyright protected. This is only for personal use. You cannot amend, distribute, sell, use, quote or paraphrase any part or the content within this book without the consent of the author.

Disclaimer: This book is a work of fanfiction; it is not an official Minecraft book. It is not endorsed, authorized, licensed, sponsored, or supported by Mojang AB, Microsoft Corp. or any other entity owning or controlling rights to the Minecraft name, trademarks or copyrights.

ISBN: 978-0-6456193-0-0

CONTENTS

Chapter 1: Just Another Sunday 7

Chapter 2: Wizzler the Wizard 14

Chapter 3: "I don't think that's Betty" 26

Chapter 4: "His body is built with weapons" 32

Chapter 5: "Is that you?" 37

Chapter 6: A wave of zombies 44

Chapter 7: "You can talk?" 52

Meet the Author 123

CHAPTER 1

JUST ANOTHER SUNDAY

"NO MINECRAFT TODAY," Mom warned as she prepared to leave for the grocery store. "You two have been glued to that game all week." She gave us one of her "looks" before closing the door behind her.

It *was* tempting to get back to it. Soooo tempting. Anyway, who would stop them? Dad?

The twins peeked into the master bedroom and realized that was unlikely. Dad was here, but he was sound asleep after working the night shift. A book was flopped onto his face. He was out.

Still, better leave Minecraft alone. Mom would find out. She always knew when they had done something they weren't supposed to. It was like she had magical powers.

Back in the living room, ten-year-olds Jack and Mindy slumped on the couch.

"No Minecraft! Ughhh. I'm bored," said Jack.

"Me too," Mindy yawned.

"What should we do?" answered Jack.

Dash, their loveable dog, barked.

Mindy smiled. "I think Dash said we should watch TV."

She grabbed the remote and turned on a football game. Mindy loved football, well, any sport really. She was the best athlete in her class and could beat anyone—boys, girls, you name it—in an arm-wrestling competition.

"No, I don't wanna watch sports!" Jack groaned. "Let's watch the science channel."

Jack snatched the remote from his sister's hands and changed the channel. Unlike his twin, Jack was in love with anything to do with science. He was the smartest kid in his class and always aced his tests.

"No fair, I wanna watch the game!" said Mindy as she grabbed the remote.

Jack pulled the remote back. "No, science."

"Sports!"

"Science!"

"Sports!"

MEET THE TOWER WIZARD

As they fought, the remote flew from their hands and went flying into the air. Time slowed down as they watched it soar closer and closer to the living room shelves, a direct line towards Mom's precious diamond figurine miniatures collection!

"Nooooo!" they shouted in unison.

Too late. The remote landed with a *clang* into an inch-high diamond figurine in the shape of a cow.

The twins watched in horror as the diamond cow fell to the floor and shattered into about a million tiny pieces—maybe more.

Mindy and Jack gasped, frozen for a second, before they recovered and went straight into blaming the other for the crisis.

JUST ANOTHER SUNDAY

"That was your fault!" accused Mindy.

"No, yours!" replied Jack.

Mindy groaned. "Mom's going to be furious! She got that for a wedding present!"

Jack sprinted out of the room, reappearing moments later, looking relieved. "I can't believe Dad slept through that noise!"

Lucky Dad WAS a deep sleeper, because suddenly Dash started barking and jumping up and down.

"Dash, be quiet, we're trying to think!" shouted Mindy.

Dash kept barking, more and more each minute, dancing in circles around the now million-pieced diamond cow.

"Is he trying to tell us something?" asked Jack.

The twins bent down and tried to calm their dog, but it was no use.

WOOF!

They stepped a little closer.

WOOF!

A little closer.

WOOF!

At the third bark the twins grabbed hold of Dash's collar in unison, and that's when something very strange happened. Everything went quiet for about a second, then, instead of being surrounded by the patterned wallpaper of their living room, they were in a big space that seemed to . . . sparkle.

"What just happened? screamed Jack.

"Jack, look at you!" exclaimed Mindy. "You're made of . . . Cubes!"

"You, too!"

CHAPTER 2

WIZZLER THE WIZARD

WOOF!

THE TWINS TURNED to look at Dash, who was now a cubed version of a dog.

"Dash, did you teleport us here?" asked Jack.

"Dash, are you magic?" asked Mindy, before realizing that while he may be magic, he still couldn't talk.

"I don't know what is going on," said Jack. "It seems like we came here when

WIZZLER THE WIZARD

we grabbed Dash's collar together. He definitely isn't a normal dog!"

The pair stopped looking at Dash, and instead, Jack turned to look at their surroundings properly for the first time.

Giant cube-shaped mountains and cubed trees appeared all around them. They looked up to see cube clouds and a cube sun. The path was lined with cube flowers and cube apples that seemed to be growing from cube trees. Mindy cried out in surprise when she spotted a bird made of cubes fly lazily past.

"Look!"

"This place is crazy," said Jack in awe.

"I know, right? It's amazing!" said Mindy.

MEET THE TOWER WIZARD

"Amazing? This place is terrifying!" corrected Jack.

"Jack, we were bored, remember? And I don't know about you, but I was just wishing we had been allowed to play more Minecraft. This is it! We are IN Minecraft! We'll never be bored here!"

"But how will we get home?" replied Jack.

"Remember that broken diamond cow figurine is still lying in the living room," he said. "All one million pieces of it. Mom will be mad if she sees that."

"Oh, you're right. Well, we'll have to find a way back home so we can clean it up before she finds out."

"But how?"

Dash did a little spin on the spot and jumped up and down.

"Dash, do *you* know how to get us home?"

Without warning, Dash turned around and took off down the hill. Mindy and Jack cried out in surprise; not only was Dash not a cube at home; he was super obedient, and, despite his busy-sounding name, chill. Nothing like his cube version.

"Wait for us, Dash!" said Jack.

The twins followed him and they ran through the thick woods and over tall mountains. Eventually they came across a giant stone tower, reaching high into the sky, way above the cube clouds.

"Wow . . . it's humongous!" exclaimed Jack.

MEET THE TOWER WIZARD

WOOF!

Dash pointed his nose towards the tower.

"Who do you think lives there?" asked Mindy.

"I don't know, but whoever it is, Dash really wants us to meet him," replied Jack.

"Maybe the owner of the tower will know how we can get back home?"

"I hope so!"

They followed Dash to the entrance of the tower. Mindy hesitated, then knocked three times on the big wooden door.

Knock, knock, knock.

"Hello? Anybody home?" she called.

WIZZLER THE WIZARD

At first there was no reply, but then a hole slid open in the door, and they heard a great, booming voice.

"Who goes there?"

Jack, Mindy, and Dash jumped in surprise at the voice and started to tremble with fear. The voice sounded so scary and deep.

Mindy, the bravest of the three, stepped forward.

"I'm Mindy. This is my twin brother, Jack, and our dog, Dash. We don't know how we got here, but somehow, we were teleported to this strange world, and we need to get home. Can you help us?"

There was a slight pause, then the door opened. Behind the door stood an old man with a great giant beard that reached his

MEET THE TOWER WIZARD

toes. He had on a purple robe featuring a dizzying pattern of bright blue stars.

"Greetings," he said in a deep, ancient voice. "I am Wizzler the Wizard. You can call me Wizzler. I am the master of this tower."

Mindy gulped. "Um, hello."

"So, you want to get back home?" asked Wizzler.

Boy, girl, and dog all nodded simultaneously, too surprised to speak (or bark).

"Fine," said Wizzler. "I will help you. Follow me."

The wizard entered the tower and started climbing the winding steps up to the top. The twins and Dash looked at each other, then shrugged. It seemed like the only option they had.

One by one they followed the wizard up the stairs.

When they reached the top floor, all four emerged into a giant room full of potions, chests, a big stone furnace, a brown crafting table, and many random objects in glass jars. It was the strangest room they had ever seen!

The wizard turned to face them. "I will help you get back home, but only if, first, you do something in return for me," he said.

"What do you want us to do?" asked Jack, stepping beside his sister bravely.

"I want you to help me find my best friend, Betty the Cow," said Wizzler.

MEET THE TOWER WIZARD

"Betty the Cow?" asked Mindy. "Your best friend is a cow?"

"Don't you underestimate Betty!" exclaimed Wizzler in an offended tone. "She's the wisest animal I've ever met."

"Okay, sorry," apologized Mindy.

"Is Betty lost?" asked Jack.

"Yes," said Wizzler. "The last time I saw her was about a week ago. She was last seen by the zombie's lair, but I don't know where she went. Here."

The wizard waved his hands and instantly a map appeared out of thin air.

"This is where we are." He jabbed a knobby finger at the map, pointing to a marking in the shape of the tower. "And this is where the zombie's lair is." He trailed his finger all the way to the top of the map, where it looked like some caves were located.

"Please help me find my friend. And in return, I'll help you find your way home."

Mindy and Jack nodded. "You can count on us," they said in unison.

The wizard chuckled. It was funny how similar yet different these twins were.

WOOF!

Dash barked and looked at the wizard meaningfully.

The wizard clapped his hands. "Oh, you're right! Here, this might help you."

Jack's eyes widened in awe. "Wait, you can understand our dog?"

MEET THE TOWER WIZARD

"Oh but of course! I can speak to all animals in these lands."

"That's amazing!"

"Yes, yes, but come on, you need to get going, Betty needs your help. Dash just reminded me of something I need to give you. "

The wizard pulled out what looked like an animal's collar from his sleeve. It had the name "Betty" on it. He offered it to Dash who took one sniff and barked before running off down the stairs.

"Dash!?" called Mindy.

The wizard smiled knowingly. "It looks like your dog friend knows what he's doing."

"But why did he leave?" asked Mindy.

Jack lifted his hand when it dawned on him. "Dash could smell Betty's scent from the collar! Come on, Mindy, we'd better hurry or he'll find Betty before we do!"

Jack hurried after Dash, followed closely by Mindy.

The wizard called after them. "Good luck."

CHAPTER 3

"I DON'T THINK THAT'S BETTY"

THE TRIO SET off across the landscape, pressing through dense cube forests and by giant cube mountains. Jack held the map while Dash led the way, until eventually they came to a giant lake. Mindy leaned at the edge of the lake and scooped a bit of water in her hands. She marveled at how the water remained in its cubed form in her hands.

"This place is out of this world!" she cried.

"You can say that again," said Jack.

"I DON'T THINK THAT'S BETTY"

Suddenly Dash lifted his head; his ears perked up in the air. He looked to the left, then right, sniffed the air once, and started to growl.

"What is it, Dash?" asked Mindy. "Is it Betty? Can you smell her?"

There was a sound like steam coming out of a kettle, followed by a gritty noise—a bit like grinding thick salt in a shaker.

"I don't think that's Betty," said Jack fearfully.

They looked around in confusion until finally, from the depths of the lake, a giant spider emerged.

"AHHHHHHHHH!" the twins screamed.

Dash started barking madly but the spider seemed unbothered by the noise, and

MEET THE TOWER WIZARD

quickly approached them. It was easily twice the twins' size and bared its fangs at them like a monster.

HSHHKKSHH!

"Run!" yelled Jack.

The twins turned around and started running, but Jack's foot got caught on a branch lying on the ground and he fell over.

Mindy stopped in her tracks. "Jack!"

"Run, go on without me!" cried Jack.

"No way!" Mindy quickly ran back to Jack and helped him up, but it was too late, the spider was right on them.

Mindy took one look at the branch and, thinking quickly, lifted it up and wacked the spider right in the face, just like in baseball practice. The spider fell over with a thud, but it wasn't finished yet, and got right back up.

While Dash distracted the spider with his barking, Mindy ran towards the spider and leapt right over it, like in high jump at school. Still not finished, she hit it again on the head. The creature's whole body suddenly flashed red. It looked like it was taking some damage.

"Mindy, watch out!" shouted Jack.

Mindy hadn't noticed but the spider was now shooting out gross strings of web. One string zoomed by, narrowly missing her. Suddenly Mindy had another idea. She started running around the spider, darting back and forth, this time as if she were playing a game of dodgeball. Dash joined in and by the time they were done, the spider had entangled himself in its own web. It hissed and tried to get free of the web trap, but it was no use.

Jack ran up to Mindy and hugged her. "That was amazing!"

"Thanks," said Mindy with a smile. "If it weren't for me, you would've been minced meat."

Jack rolled his eyes. "Yeah, yeah, no need to get so cocky about it."

Mindy laughed and Dash jumped up and down.

"Oh, and you were amazing too, Dash!" said Mindy.

She patted his head, and he licked her hand.

"Ew, gross!"

Mindy and Jack laughed while Dash leapt into the air again like a kangaroo.

A few minutes later, after Dash had finally calmed down, the twins and their dog set off again on their journey.

CHAPTER 4

"HIS BODY IS BUILT WITH WEAPONS"

AFTER WALKING FOR a long time, they finally stumbled upon the large opening to a cave. Outside it was day, but inside the cave looked as dark as Dash's little black nose.

"So, is this the zombie's lair?" asked Mindy.

"It must be," replied Jack, examining the map. He glanced up. "Do you think there are real zombies in there?"

"HIS BODY IS BUILT WITH WEAPONS"

"If this world is anything like the Minecraft game, then there definitely will be," said Mindy. "Which is why we need to arm ourselves with some weapons."

"You're right," Jack nodded. "We should harvest some wood and get crafting."

Together, the twins headed off towards a clump of trees. They started hitting at the tree bark with their hands. It took a while, but eventually they managed to gather a good heap of wood. Dash sniffed the timber and looked up at them in confusion, as if to say, *"What are you two doing?"*

"We're making some wooden swords, Dash," said Jack. "But first we need some wooden planks."

Jack set up the blocks of wood on the ground which suddenly transformed into several wooden planks, as if by magic.

MEET THE TOWER WIZARD

"Perfect! And if I remember correctly from my time playing Minecraft, if I position these like this . . ." Jack stacked the planks next to one another. Suddenly the two wooden planks disappeared and were replaced by four sticks.

Mindy clapped her hands in excitement as Dash jumped around and barked like crazy.

"Yes!" cried Jack with glee. "And now for the final step . . ."

He moved one wooden plank so it was at the bottom, then laid two sticks on the ground beside it. Low and behold, the sticks and wooden plank vanished and instead a wooden sword appeared!

"Woohoo!" shouted Mindy. She grabbed a hold of Dash's front paws, and they started dancing together with joy.

"HIS BODY IS BUILT WITH WEAPONS"

Jack did the same thing again so now he and Mindy had a wooden sword each.

"And now . . ." He lifted his sword into the air. "We're ready to face the zombie's lair."

WOOF!

"Oh wait, I forgot, do you need anything, Dash?" asked Jack, apologetically.

WOOF!

"I don't know what he's saying." Jack looked to Mindy for help.

She shrugged. "He should be fine. He's a dog after all. He has his teeth and his claws. His body is already built with weapons for defending himself."

"You're right," nodded Jack. "Well, into the zombie's lair we go!"

MEET THE TOWER WIZARD

They headed through the cave's entrance, right into the darkness.

CHAPTER 5

"IS THAT YOU?"

INSIDE THE CAVE the air was much cooler and sent tingling chills down their spines.

Mindy shivered. "Why is it so cold?"

"They're zombies," said Jack. "They love the cold and dark."

"*Brrr*... I would hate to be a zombie," said Mindy. "Jack, if you ever turn into a zombie, promise me you won't bite me and turn me into one, too."

"If I'm a zombie I won't even know who you are," scoffed Jack.

MEET THE TOWER WIZARD

Mindy gasped. "How rude!"

Jack giggled, but in the eerie caves, his laughter echoed out and returned to them like strange wails. He glanced around and noticed there was lots of coal stuck in the walls.

Mindy and Jack wordlessly held hands as they ventured deeper and deeper into the maze of caves. Before long, it got so dark that they could hardly see each other.

Suddenly Jack felt something hard and cold touch his left shoulder.

"Mindy . . . Is that you?" he asked nervously.

"No, I'm over here," came her voice, over from his right.

"Dash, is that you?"

"IS THAT YOU?"

WOOF! came Dash's voice, but that was from in front of him.

"Wait—if it's not you, Mindy. And it's not Dash, then . . ."

Jack turned around and yelled out when he spotted the zombie right behind him!

"**AHHHHHH!**" he shouted.

The zombie's skin was wilted and green, and it made Jack's stomach turn over in disgust. He backed away as the zombie creeped towards him, closer and closer, groaning in a gravelly voice. It seemed to be saying the word "**ZOMBIE**". It reached out towards him as if to offer a hug, but Jack knew better.

The twins kept the zombies back with their swords, and Dash barked loudly as if he wanted to bring the whole cavern

MEET THE TOWER WIZARD

down. It was no use. Pretty soon, a swarm of zombies surrounded them. They were getting overwhelmed—there was no way just three of them could face off an army of zombies.

As the zombies backed them into a corner, Jack and Mindy looked around. Suddenly, they noticed Dash wasn't with them anymore.

"Where did Dash go? He didn't abandon us, did he?" asked Mindy in shock.

"No way, Dash would never do that!" said Jack.

They looked around in confusion, then heard a bark from above. Dash was standing on a kind of ledge above them.

"IS THAT YOU?"

"Quick, let's climb up. The zombies might have a hard time following us up there," said Jack.

Mindy and Jack started to climb the blocks of stone until they reached the ledge where Dash stood. The zombies tried to follow but it was no use; they couldn't climb up. Dash's quick thinking had gained them a few minutes of rest, but now they had a new problem: how were they going to get out of there?

"Jack, what do we do?" asked Mindy desperately.

Jack wracked his brain for a solution. This was Minecraft. He played it almost every day after school. Surely, he could think of something.

Then it hit him. Fire. Zombies hated fire!

MEET THE TOWER WIZARD

"Quick, someone get me some coal!" said Jack.

"From where?" asked Mindy.

"The cave walls. There's coal in the rock!" he said.

Mindy quickly used her sword to hack away at the stone until finally she got some coal.

"Got it!" she shouted.

She tossed it over to Jack.

"Dash, pass me the spare sticks we had left over from before," ordered Jack.

WOOF!

Dash brought him some sticks in his mouth and Jack grabbed them. He laid out the sticks, one at the bottom, and a piece of coal above it. Like magic, the objects disappeared and in their place were two torches!

"Jack, you're a genius!"

"Quick, grab one and let's get outta here!"

CHAPTER 6

A WAVE OF ZOMBIES

MINDY GRABBED HER own torch and Jack grabbed his, then together they faced the wave of zombies.

GRGRRRGGRRR!

The zombies hissed and growled, but they didn't come any closer. Jack's plan worked! The zombies retreated back into the dark corners of the cave, away from the bright fire.

Mindy laughed loudly. "Ha! That's right. Back away, you stupid zombies!"

"Mindy, don't tease them!" cried Jack.

As he spoke, one zombie sneaked around behind the twins. It was just about to take a bite at Mindy's ankle, when Dash leaped onto it and smacked it away with his paw.

WOOF!

"Woah, that was a close one," gasped Mindy. "Thanks Dash."

Eventually they managed to make it out of the cave, back into the safe, warm sunlight. The zombies followed them to the edge of the cave, but suddenly stopped, refusing to move any further.

Jack looked up at the sun and soaked the warmth in.

He sighed with relief. "We made it."

MEET THE TOWER WIZARD

"We still have to find Betty," said Mindy. "All we've managed so far is nearly getting eaten by a spider and a swarm of zombies."

"You're right," groaned Jack. "What can we do now? The wizard said the last time he saw Betty was by the zombie's lair, and we're here but so far, we've seen no sign of her."

"There has to be some way," said Mindy. "We can't give up!"

While the twins sat down on the grass and tried to think of something, Dash wandered over to look out over the landscape. Suddenly a rogue wind drifted by. Dash sniffed at the wind and his ears perked up. He recognized that smell! It was the smell of Betty the Cow! Dash turned back to the twins in excitement, desperate to tell them what he had discovered.

Mindy, Jack, I know where Betty is, he thought, but instead all that came out was a short WOOF!

"What is it, boy?" said Mindy.

"Are you hungry? Do you wanna play fetch?" asked Jack.

"Now's not the time to play fetch, Dash!" scolded Mindy.

Dash barked again in frustration, trying to make them understand, but it was no use. They couldn't speak dog language.

Woof, he barked sadly.

In an instant, genius struck. He realized he didn't need to *tell* them. He could just *show* them!

WOOF! He barked. *Follow me!*

MEET THE TOWER WIZARD

Then he turned and took off running across the field.

"Dash?!" shouted Mindy.

"Quick, after him!" called Jack.

The twins followed their dog as he led them through a giant forest. They darted in and out of the cube-shaped trees, past a small family of pink pigs, through a field of cube poppies. Finally, Dash came to a stop at the bottom of a mountain.

Jack collapsed to the ground, panting, and struggling for air.

"That . . ." gasped Jack, "was . . . a . . . long . . ." He took a quick breath. "Journey."

"Where are we, Dash?" asked Mindy, who, as the sportier twin, had far better stamina than Jack.

WOOF!

Dash pointed with his nose to the mountain rising tall above them, reaching high into the clouds.

"You want us to climb? All the way up there?!" exclaimed Mindy.

"Please, no more running. I need to sleep!" complained Jack.

Mindy looked up at the mountain, then down at Dash.

Dash nodded as if to say, *trust me*.

"Alright, I trust you, Dash," she said. Then she turned to Jack. "Come on."

MEET THE TOWER WIZARD

"Noooo!" he moaned.

"Come on, we have to find Betty!"

Mindy helped Jack to his feet and together they began the challenging climb up the mountain. It was hard work climbing over each block. Their knees ached, their backs ached, their necks ached—everything ached!

Dash, on the other hand, seemed to be having the time of his life. He leaped onto the blocks, climbing higher and higher, making it look like a piece of cake.

When they were halfway and Jack really felt like giving up, Dash worked even harder. He nudged Jack encouragingly with his snout, and practically pushed him up the mountain until Jack had enough energy to finish the climb himself.

Eventually, after about two hours, they made it to the top. What they found there shocked them to their core.

CHAPTER 7

"YOU CAN TALK?"

"WHAT ON EARTH is that?" exclaimed Jack.

They gazed in astonishment at the giant portal before them. It was bordered by smooth, black blocks of what looked like stone, except what they were looking at seemed much heavier.

The blocks were stacked into the outline of a rectangle, rising high above them. Inside the rectangle was a weird shimmery purple *thing*. Whatever it was moved and swayed in the air, distorting the view behind it.

"YOU CAN TALK?"

As the twins stepped closer, within the surface of the portal they could see small sparks flying off the purple object, and lilac-colored spirals spinning in the purple abyss. It was unlike anything they had ever seen before.

"I don't like it," said Mindy, backing away.

"It definitely looks like a portal," said Jack in awe.

"It looks scary," replied Mindy.

WOOF! said Dash.

Jack looked from Dash, to the portal, then back to Dash.

"Wait . . . is Betty in *there*?" he asked in shock.

MEET THE TOWER WIZARD

"Why would a cow go through that . . .thing?" asked Mindy.

"I don't know, but Dash seems to be certain she's in there," said Jack. "Well . . . are you ready?"

Mindy took a deep breath, raised her wooden sword, and nodded. "I'm ready."

"Dash?"

Dash did a spin and barked.

"I'll take that as a yes."

Jack raised his own wooden sword and eyed the swirling purple portal. "Let's do this."

Together they ran and leaped into the portal.

"YOU CAN TALK?"

It felt like every bone was bending at odd angles; like their organs were dancing in their bodies. After what seemed like ages, but also not long at all, they emerged on the other side of the portal.

"Nooooo...waaaay," gasped Mindy.

Before them lay the Nether. A giant world of fire and chaos.

All around them waterfalls of lava cascaded into giant lava lakes. The earth here was a deep, dark red. It reminded Jack of his mother's darkest shade of lipstick. Above them, more and more of that deep, dark red stone lined the ceiling. Of course, there was no sky in the Nether.

The air was full of sparks of fire that had floated off the lava, and when it landed on them it stung like a painful ant bite.

"Ow, that hurts!" yelped Jack.

"This place is unreal," Mindy gazed around in awe.

"It's terrifying," mumbled Jack.

Mindy started to walk forward but Jack noticed something and immediately pulled her back to hide behind a wall.

"Hey, what's the big deal?" said Mindy.

"Shh!" Jack whispered. "Look."

He pointed to the creatures that roamed the ground far below them. Jack recognized them from his hours of playing Minecraft after school.

There were the Piglins: humanoid pigs that looked like they were possessed by a kind of ghost. From here, they looked docile

"YOU CAN TALK?"

enough, but Jack knew if even one Piglin spotted them, they would be toast.

To make it worse, there were also Ghasts: giant squid-like creatures that floated lazily through the sky. Jack knew their laziness was deceptive. A ghast could shoot fireballs at you without even raising a tentacle.

Finally, he spotted a few Zombified Piglins. This strange creature, which looked like a mix between a zombie and a pig (albeit one with vines growing across its body) was pretty peaceful—so long as it wasn't attacked.

All these creatures lay before them. All of them capable of attacking the twins and their beloved dog.

"We have to be very, *very* quiet." Jack began.

Too late. It seemed Mindy had other plans. Without warning, she stood up and raised her sword, shouting a war cry.

"Fear me!" she shouted, as she leapt off the ledge and charged at the creatures.

"MINDY, NO!" screamed Jack.

But there was no stopping Mindy once she had her mind set on something. She charged at the creatures and began knocking them down in quick succession with her sword.

Mindy was amazing, but there were just so many of them. Jack had no choice but to join her, and together they swung at Piglins and Ghasts until their arms ached with exhaustion. Dash joined them, too, biting at the ankles of the Nether creatures, but the situation soon started to feel overwhelming.

"YOU CAN TALK?"

More and more creatures kept arriving.

Still, the trio persevered.

Over her shoulder, Mindy spotted another Zombified Piglin. (Where were they all coming from?) She took aim, but then gasped in horror as her wooden sword started to disintegrate in her hands. Within a few seconds, she was left holding nothing but empty air.

"My sword!" she cried.

Jack took another swing at a Piglin and sure enough, his sword disintegrated as well. Their weapons had been used up to the max. Not only were they stuck in the Nether, but the twins were weaponless!

"Oh no!" he cried.

MEET THE TOWER WIZARD

The creatures cornered them, and it seemed this was truly the end of their great adventure in the Minecraft world. Suddenly, a booming sound seemed to be calling out to them.

MOOOOOOOOOOO!!!

They looked up above them to see a cow standing at the top of a hill.

"Is that . . . Betty?" cried Mindy.

The black and white cow wore a great big diamond helmet with sharp horns.

"I'm coming!" called Betty in a low female voice.

"**YOU CAN TALK?!**" shouted Jack in bewilderment.

"YOU CAN TALK?"

Betty took off down the hill at full gallop and rammed her head into the crowd of creatures. Zombified Piglins, Piglins, and Ghasts alike flew into the air, knocked away by the sheer force of Betty's head.

Pretty quickly she made her way through the mass of creatures, carving a path through them, until finally she came to a stop in front of the stunned twins and dog.

"Howdy," she said.

Her accent sounded like a cowgirl the twins had seen in a movie once. Except, she had been a *girl*, not an actual cow!

"B-Betty?" stammered Jack.

"That's me," replied Betty with a low curtsy, but it looked funny since she was a cow.

MEET THE TOWER WIZARD

"I didn't know cows could talk here," said Mindy.

Betty grinned. "Oh, no they usually can't, but I have a friend, he's a wizard actually, and he did some magic and gave me the power to talk!"

Jack smacked his head. He couldn't believe he had forgotten the whole reason why they were here! "Oh, that reminds me—the wizard sent us here to save you!"

"Save me?" asked Betty with a frown. "Why would I need saving?"

Jack frowned as well, confused. "Well, because he said you've been missing for days, and—"

Betty suddenly laughed out loud—a low, rumbling laugh that felt a little contagious and made Dash bark with glee.

"YOU CAN TALK?"

"Missing?" snorted Betty. "I told him I was coming here to mine some Quartz! I even left him a note. That wizard's losing his memory by the day."

"So . . . we came all this way for nothing?" said Mindy sadly.

"Oh, don't be sad little one. I'll make sure you get a nice reward for your good deed and—a"

But before the cow could say anything further, a giant red creature with bony wings swooped in and grabbed Betty, lifting her into the air.

"AHHHHH!" she screamed, as Mindy, Jack, and Dash stood in shock, too stunned to even move.

MEET THE TOWER WIZARD

"Betty!" cried Jack finally, but the winged creature took off with Betty, up to the top of a giant fortress far away in the distance.

"Quick, we have to save her!" said Mindy, taking off on a run.

"Looks like this has turned into a rescue mission after all," said Jack, following in her footsteps.

They weaved through the bodies of the Nether creatures, all knocked unconscious by Betty's great horns, and, careful not to tread on any fingers, they headed towards the monstrous fortress.

It seemed this adventure was far from over.

⬛ ⬛ ⬛

Jack, Mindy, and Dash ran across the Nether, the ground hot beneath their feet.

"YOU CAN TALK?"

Most of the creatures had been scared away by Betty's attack, and so they had a clear path to the fortress. Ahead of them, the fortress loomed above like a humongous wave, made of the same purplish-red stone, but it seemed to be more solid and strong. There were two spires, a big wall around the perimeter, a five-meter-high entryway, and a tall tower at the center. That was where the red winged creature had taken Betty.

"Come on, this way," called Jack, leading the others through the gate.

Inside, it seemed almost too quiet. The fortress was deserted. It seemed the only Nether creature that lived here was that big, winged thing that had taken Betty.

The trio raced into the main building at the center. They came upon three pathways.

MEET THE TOWER WIZARD

"Which one goes to the tower?" asked Mindy in a panic.

"I don't know," replied Jack.

"Should we split up?"

"No! We need to stick together."

"But Betty needs us! If we split up, we'll get to her faster."

"No Mindy, if we split up then one of us could get really hurt."

As the twins bickered and argued over what to do, Dash went over and sniffed at each of the paths. He sniffed and sniffed, and suddenly he got the smallest whiff of a smell he recognized—Betty!

Woof!

"YOU CAN TALK?"

The twins ignored him, still arguing loudly. Their faces were hot with all their shouting.

WOOF!

He barked again, much louder this time, and finally they stopped to turn to him.

"**WHAT?**" they shouted in unison, feeling stressed.

Dash smiled with his tongue out and led them up the middle path. Mincy and Jack looked at each other and shrugged.

"He seems to know what he's doing," noted Jack.

The twins followed Dash up the stairs, and sure enough the path started to lead them higher and higher, towards the tall tower. It was dizzying going round and round up the staircase, so every now and then they

MEET THE TOWER WIZARD

took a break where a tiny window was cut into the wall. From the window they had a view of the whole Nether: all the monstrous creatures, the eerie red sky, the pit of burning lava. Mindy shuddered when she realized just how high they were. She wasn't scared of a lot of things, but heights were one of her few phobias.

Up and up, they climbed. Up and up and up, until finally they reached a big oak door with a brass door handle.

"I think this is it," panted Jack.

"Too bad we don't have any weapons," moaned Mindy.

Dash gently nudged her hand, and Mindy patted his head fondly.

"Oh yes, how could I forget—we have you, Dash!" she whispered.

"YOU CAN TALK?"

Jack turned to Mindy and Dash.

"Ready?" he asked quietly.

They nodded. Jack took a deep breath and opened the door.

Inside, it was a most peculiar sight indeed. Betty was trapped in a big cage in one corner of the room, steel bars blocking her from freedom. Ahead, a wide window, attached to a balcony, provided a view of the fiery scenery below. Redstone lined the walls, floor, and ceiling. There was a small bed, a table, and some chairs. If the cow in the cage wasn't strange enough, then the winged creature sitting at the table certainly topped it all off.

The creature guarding Betty appeared to be something like a bat, except it was easily the size of a car. It had red leathery skin, and on its wings its bones poked

MEET THE TOWER WIZARD

out like spikes, white and steely. From its backside protruded a short scorpion's tail, with a stinger at the end that seemed like it could deal a lot of damage. From the way the animal was seated at the desk they could see the underside of its belly, which looked oddly soft and squishy, like the underbelly of a cat when it rolled over on its side. But by the way this creature looked and moved, the twins could tell it was much more dangerous than a cat.

The creature looked up at them and seemed to appear shocked.

"Who are you?" he asked.

His voice sounded like sandpaper and echoed out across the room, banging the insides of their brains. When the twins gave no reply, the creature got up from the desk and slinked towards them. The twins

"YOU CAN TALK?"

started to tremble with fear, while Betty shouted at the creature.

"You stay away from those kids!" she yelled fiercely.

Dash barked at the creature like crazy, but the winged beast took one look at the dog, laughed to itself, then lifted his wing and grabbed Dash as if he weighed nothing.

"No! Leave Dash alone!" yelled the twins, but the creature ignored them and placed Dash into the cell with Betty.

Mindy ran over and banged her fists at the creature's side, but he just looked at her and laughed deeply, a low rumble that started in his belly then rose into his throat like an earthquake.

"That tickles," he said.

MEET THE TOWER WIZARD

Then, to Jack's horror, the creature lifted Mindy up and threw her into the cage as well!

"**MINDY!**" screamed Jack.

Hot, red anger coursed through his veins, and he leapt at the creature with just his fists.

"**LET. HER. GO!**" he shouted.

But the creature looked at him and promptly placed him in the cage as well.

Mindy hugged Jack tightly. "Thanks for trying."

The creature turned and locked his spooky, pure white eyes on the group of prisoners. They all backed away in fear.

"You amuse me," he said. "I'll keep you all as my little pets."

And with that he leapt off the balcony and soared away.

"That's right, you better fly away!" called Jack weakly.

Mindy gave him a supporting pat on the back, then collapsed on the ground.

"Well, I guess we're doomed to spend the rest of our lives here now," she said sadly.

"No! Don't give up hope!" said Jack. "We'll make it out of here."

"How?"

"Um . . . we'll break the steel bars!"

"They're too strong."

MEET THE TOWER WIZARD

"Then . . . we'll call for help!"

"Who can we call?" Mindy asked. "This place is full of monsters and enemies. No one is here to help us."

"Well, what about Wizzler the Wizard? He could save us!"

"Didn't you hear what Betty said? He's forgetful. He probably forgot he even sent us on a rescue mission."

"Then . . . then . . ." Jack sighed then plonked on the ground beside her. "I guess you're right. We're stuck here forever."

"I miss Mom and Dad," said Mindy in a low voice.

"Me, too," replied Jack mournfully.

"YOU CAN TALK?"

They were quiet for a while. The air was very still—not even the sound of a Piglin's war cry could be heard. Dash walked over and lay between the twins. They each hugged him for comfort. Betty watched the sad trio thoughtfully.

"Well, we may not know a way out just yet," said Betty, laying down and tucking her hooves underneath her. "But if there's one thing I know for certain, it's that we'll find a way out of here, one way or another. Everything works out in the end."

"But how do you know that?" asked Mindy.

Betty winked. The action looked funny on a cow and brought a small smile on the twins faces.

"I just know," said Betty firmly.

MEET THE TOWER WIZARD

The twins took a deep breath and nodded. Betty was happy to see their spirits had been lifted, at least a little.

"Well, it looks like we may be here for some time, so why don't we get to know each other?" asked Betty.

Jack nodded. "I'm Jack, and this is my twin sister, Mindy." Jack patted Dash on the head. "And this is our dog, Dash."

"Oh yes, I know who Dash is," said Betty.

"You do?" said the twins in unison.

"Dash travels here very often," she said.

The twins turned to Dash, who looked away sheepishly.

"Dash, who *are* you?" asked Mindy in wonder.

"YOU CAN TALK?"

Dash turned to them with wise eyes and gave a small bark. It seemed the twins would never find out who exactly their trusted companion was. But perhaps sometime in the future they would discover the secrets of his past.

Jack turned to Betty. "And what about you? Tell us about yourself."

Betty smiled, and somehow in this world, a smile on a cow looked quite normal. "Well, you already know my name. I'm Betty the Cow. I was born over by the Grazing Field, far, far away from here. I studied mathematics and got a master's degree, and—a"

"Woah, woah, woah," said Mindy, raising her hands in confusion. "Slow down. You went to university? Cows can do that?"

MEET THE TOWER WIZARD

"Oh yes," said Betty. "I have a feeling the cows in this world are very different from the cows in your world."

While the twins tried to wrap their heads around the idea of a cow studying at university, Betty continued.

"I graduated from university and decided I wanted to explore the world and go on crazy adventures. So, I headed off into the unknown, and one day I came upon a village that had been ransacked by some Piglins. While I was out in a remote forest tracking down their footprints, I heard a noise and I discovered an old man in a weird costume lying on the ground."

"Wizzler the Wizard!" cried Jack in recognition.

Betty nodded. "Yes, it was our wizardly friend. He was asleep and I figured I

"YOU CAN TALK?"

should help him since there were Piglins loose in the forest. It wasn't safe. But when I went to wake him up, he shot to his feet and started yelling at me!"

"Why would he do that?" asked Mindy.

"Because supposedly he had been fake sleeping! He wanted a Piglin to try to attack him, and then Wizzler would turn the tables on the Piglin and capture him! But I had foiled his plans because I thought he was just a helpless old man who fell asleep in the forest."

"Then what happened?" asked Jack.

"Then Wizzler yelled at me a little more, so I . . . headbutted him in the stomach."

"You did?!" asked Mindy in awe.

MEET THE TOWER WIZARD

"Yep. He seemed to realize I wasn't any normal cow. You see, at this point, I didn't have the ability to speak. No one could understand me. But when the wizard realized I was special, he gifted me with a voice."

"Wow, that's amazing," said Jack, all wide-eyed. He wondered if he could do magic like the wizard someday!

"It is pretty amazing," admitted Betty. "And, once I could speak, I told him about my mission to locate the Piglins and send them back to the Nether. Wizzler agreed to help me. So, we became a team, and together we fought an epic battle against the Piglins." A wistful look passed over Betty's face. "It was truly a magnificent battle. You should've been there."

Dash barked in annoyance.

"YOU CAN TALK?"

"Oh yes, sorry, Dash, I forgot you were there, too!" said Betty.

The twins looked at Dash again in astonishment. They were learning something new about him by the minute!

"We won the battle, of course," continued Betty. "And Wizzler and I have been companions ever since. He's gotten a little cuckoo over the years but he's still my best friend."

"That was such a good story," said Mindy, her eyes bright with admiration. "I want to grow up to be someone like you someday!"

"A cow?" teased Jack.

Mindy rolled her eyes at him. "Not a cow, you jokester! You know what I mean."

"That's very sweet of you," said Betty.

MEET THE TOWER WIZARD

"And what about Wizzler?" asked Jack. "What's his story?"

Betty looked away. "I think that's a story for another time. And it's probably best if Wizzler tells you himself."

Mindy nodded in understanding. "Okay . . . well what about Dash, then?"

Betty smiled. "That's for Dash to tell you."

The twins sighed in exasperation. "But Dash can't speak!"

Dash licked their cheeks, and the twins wiped them in disgust, complaining loudly. Betty chuckled. What a funny trio they were.

//

They were imprisoned for five days. The winged creature who was their captor

"YOU CAN TALK?"

only ever came during the evening to bring them food, like apples, bread, and sometimes if they were lucky, roasted chicken. They ate the food and remained in their cage, utterly bored.

Mindy was particularly restless. She was always used to moving about, but in the confines of the cage, they were all squished within a meter of each other. Mindy decided to pass the time doing pull ups from the bars of the cage above them.

". . . 5 . . . 6 . . . 7 . . ." she puffed.

"We've been here for ages now," mumbled Jack. "Mom and Dad will be so worried."

"And so mad," cut in Mindy, landing beside him.

"Oh, don't you worry about that," said Betty suddenly. "Time works differently

MEET THE TOWER WIZARD

here. For you it's been a few days; for your parents, it's only been a few minutes.

While the twins tried to wrap their heads around that, a strong wind blasted into the tower room and whipped their hair in the air. The winged creature had arrived, bringing his massive deep red body into the room, but this time he had no food with him.

"Where's the food?" called Jack in concern.

The creature glanced at him. "No food today," he said in his dark voice.

"But we have to eat!" cried Mindy. "We need food to live!"

The creature shrugged, his bony shoulders rising up and down carelessly. "Oh well."

"YOU CAN TALK?"

And with that the creature grabbed some objects from his desk drawer and took off from the balcony, flying into the red skies of the Nether once again.

Mindy collapsed on the ground, her head in her hands. "Oh no. Oh no oh no oh no. We're done for!"

"Don't worry Mindy, we'll find a way out," said Jack, wrapping an arm around her.

"How? We've been trying to think of a way out of here for days, but we haven't even gotten close!"

"I don't know, but don't lose hope! We'll find a way."

"How do you know that?" shouted Mindy angrily. "Stop saying things just to make me feel better!"

MEET THE TOWER WIZARD

"But Mindy—"

Suddenly Betty stepped forward. "Guys, look." She pointed with her hoof at the desk drawer, the one the winged creature had just opened. A key rested inside. It probably unlocked their cage! This was the chance they were looking for to escape!

"Wait, but how can we get it?" wondered Jack out loud. "It's all the way over there!"

"We need something long; something so we can grab it from here," said Betty.

They all tried to think for a while on what to do, then a lightbulb lit up in Jack's head.

"Your collars!" he said excitedly, pointing to the collar on Dash's neck, as well as the old one they had of Betty's.

"Oh my gosh, that's perfect!" said Mindy.

"YOU CAN TALK?"

Jack unfastened Dash's collar then tied it to the end to Betty's collar. The two collars were strong enough to work like a stick.

"Here goes nothing," said Jack.

He lifted the makeshift stick and leaned out of the cage as far as he could. The stick *just* reached the desk drawer. But the key wouldn't magically attach itself to the end of the collar. It wasn't working.

"Wait, bring it back here," said Betty.

Jack pulled it back then Betty raised her mouth to the end of the stick and promptly licked it with her big purple tongue. Mindy shivered slightly—that was a *bit* too gross for her.

Jack inspected the end of the collar. Betty's saliva was super sticky, and it was just what they needed!

MEET THE TOWER WIZARD

"Awesome!" he said.

He leaned out and raised the makeshift stick again. This time the key stuck to the collar! He quickly reeled it back in while the others chattered in excitement. But at the last second, the key fell off. The saliva wasn't sticky enough!

"No! We were so close!" groaned Betty.

But then Mindy stepped forward. "Hold on, I think I can reach it with my toe."

Mindy, who was super flexible, sat down and reached her leg through the bars of the cage. She stretched as far as she could until her pinky toe brushed against the key. Slowly, carefully, she dragged it back to them. Jack quickly snatched the key from the ground before anything else could foil their plans.

"YOU CAN TALK?"

"Yes!" he cried.

They all shouted and gasped in relief, but suddenly there was a voice behind them.

"What are you all excited about?" said the deep voice.

Jack froze in horror. The winged creature. When had he returned? They must've been too distracted by the key to notice him fly into the tower room. Mindy, quick thinking, grabbed the key from Jack's hand and hid it in her shoe.

"Oh, you're back!" said Mindy in a high-pitched voice.

"Yes, I'm back," the creature echoed. Luckily, he didn't notice the missing key. "I brought you food."

MEET THE TOWER WIZARD

The creature lugged a sack from behind and gave them a few apples and pieces of bread.

"Oh," said Betty, surprised. "Why?"

"Well . . ." The creature seemed a little embarrassed. "You're my pets, and I look after my pets."

"Wow, um . . . thanks!" said Jack awkwardly, hoping the creature would leave.

But the creature seemed like he wanted to stay. He sat down and began talking to them.

"I want to get to know my pets," he said firmly.

Betty was annoyed that the creature kept calling them his "pets", but she, too,

"YOU CAN TALK?"

was surprised by his sudden change in behavior. Maybe he was feeling a little lonely?

"You," the creature pointed suddenly with his claws. "The short-haired one."

"Me?" asked Jack fearfully.

"Yes. What do you call yourself?"

"You mean, what's my name?"

"Yes, your name."

"Jack."

The creature closed his eyes. "Now you are called Chikaluka."

Mindy burst out laughing. "I like that name. Chikaluka. It suits you," she teased, wiping tears from her eyes.

The creature turned to her. "And you are named what?"

"Mindy."

The creature shook his head. "No, now you are named Poopia."

This time Jack burst out laughing, while Mindy looked offended.

"Poopia!" cried Jack, holding at the sides of his stomach as laughter rumbled through his body. "Poopia suits you, too!"

The creature watched them in amusement. "What is this sound you're making?"

"This?" asked Jack, laughing slightly. "I'm laughing."

"Laugh–ing?"

"YOU CAN TALK?"

"Yes." Betty frowned. "Have you never laughed before?"

The creature shook his head.

"I don't know how."

"Well, it's like this," said Betty, and she walked up to Mindy and licked her right on the face.

"UGH!" screamed Mindy in disgust. "GROSS!"

The creature opened his mouth and a strange electric cackle sound from his belly.

"Yes, that is funny!" he said.

Betty grinned. "Now what's *your* name?" she asked.

MEET THE TOWER WIZARD

"Me? I do not have a name," the creature replied in surprise.

"Well . . . now you are named . . . um . . ." Betty looked around for inspiration on a name.

Suddenly Dash barked.

"Ooh, that's a good one, Dash!" said Betty. She turned back to the creature. "You are now called Red."

"Red?"

"Yes. Like the color."

The creature seemed to think for a moment. "Red. I like it. Yes, my name is Red now."

"Great!" said Betty.

"YOU CAN TALK?"

Red glanced at them then stood up suddenly. "I will get you more food," he said, turning to leave. He hesitated and looked at them again. "Thank you."

And with that he heaved his wings and disappeared.

Jack cleared his throat. "Well, that was unexpected."

"You can say that again," agreed Betty.

Mindy flicked the saliva off her face with a look of pain. "Why did you have to do that, Betty?"

"Oops!" Betty grinned and helped Mindy clean her face. "Sorry!"

//

MEET THE TOWER WIZARD

As soon as Red flew away and was well out of sight, the group got to work. Mindy unlocked the cage with the key, and they all ran out with glee.

"Freedom! Finally!" cried Jack, raising his arms into the air.

"Not so fast," warned Betty. "We still have to get through the Nether with all of its deadly creatures."

"Oh yeah," said Jack. "I forgot about that."

"How will we get through?" asked Mindy.

"Well, I still have my diamond helmet," offered Betty. "Perhaps that will be enough."

"I don't think it will," Mindy replied. "We need weapons. Let's see if there are any lying around here."

"YOU CAN TALK?"

They searched through Red's belongings for anything they could use as a weapon but found nothing.

"Aw man!" groaned Mindy.

"I didn't think we'd find a weapon," admitted Betty. "After all, Red is a giant winged creature with claws. What would he need weapons for?"

"You're right, but still, I was hopeful," Mindy sighed.

"Come on," said Jack. "Let's get out of here before he finds out we escaped."

The others nodded. Together they rushed down the spiraling staircase and out the front door of the tower (luckily it was unlocked), through the courtyard of the fortress, and back out into the dry lands of the Nether. As soon as they were on bare ground again, heat blasted them with the force of a hurricane.

"How can these creatures survive in a place like this?" asked Mindy as they ran. "It's horrible!"

"Nether creatures are very strange," noted Jack.

They ran and ran until they reached a giant hill.

"Where's the portal that brought you here?" asked Betty.

"I don't know!" said Jack, suddenly panicked.

"Maybe we'll spot it from up there," said Mindy, pointing to the hill.

"YOU CAN TALK?"

They climbed until they reached the very top, and from here they had a wide sweeping view of all of the Nether.

Jack panted heavily, tired from climbing. "I can't see the portal."

"Is that it?" pointed Mindy.

"No, that's just a purple cloud."

They continued searching until suddenly Betty cried out in joy. "Found it!"

She pointed with her hoof and the twins cheered. There was the portal, nestled between two giant boulders. It was tricky to see. Betty must have some really good cow eyes.

"It's not that far away!" exclaimed Jack. "We might actually survive this!"

MEET THE TOWER WIZARD

But then a fog they hadn't noticed before drifted away, revealing the hidden ugly sight beneath it, and their hearts fell into the pits of their stomach. Dozens if not hundreds of the enemy laid between them and the portal. Piglins, Ghasts, and Zombified Piglins roamed the ground, searching for their next prey.

Jack, Mindy, Dash, and Betty hunched low on the ground in fear. They had to keep very still so they weren't spotted.

"Everyone stay very, very quiet," whispered Jack.

They waited, searching for an answer, but then suddenly they heard a sound. A low rumble came from the base of Betty's body, rose along her back, until finally, it emerged as a loud, echoing fart!

Mindy gasped. "Betty!" she complained.

"I'm sorry," said Betty, flushed with embarrassment. "I can't help it. I'm a cow!"

The twins, the dog, and the cow glanced at the creatures below. Each stared back at them.

Jack gulped. "Run!"

They took off, but the evil creatures of the Nether were soon close on their heels.

"We should at least try to make it to the portal!" shouted Mindy over the pounding of the stampede behind them.

"Let's make a long U-turn," shouted Jack. "Maybe we can cut them off and make it through the portal!"

They ran as fast as they could but there were just so many of them. Betty remained

MEET THE TOWER WIZARD

at the back to knock away any creatures that got too close with her diamond helmet. She felt guilty because her stomach was the whole reason why they were in this mess. But even Betty was having trouble keeping the creatures at bay.

Eventually Jack led them around a corner and froze in horror. A giant cliff wall faced them, blocking the way. It was impossible to climb. It was as flat and high as a skyscraper. They were trapped.

"Oh no!" cried Mindy in dismay.

They tried to turn back but the horde of Piglins, Ghasts, and Zombified Piglins blocked their way. Betty held them off as best she could, but there were just too many of them. Jack turned to Mindy and took her hands. This was it. Their adventure was over . . .

"YOU CAN TALK?"

Or so they thought!

Suddenly from above there was a loud roar, and a great red creature flew down, landing between the group and the evil creatures with a big force of wind.

"Red?!" yelled Betty in surprise.

Red turned to look at them. It looked like he was smiling.

"Don't worry, Red is here to save you!"

Red turned to the smaller Nether creatures and let out another mighty roar. It was so loud Mindy and Jack had to plug their ears. The Piglins, Ghasts, and Zombified Piglins took one look at each other then took off running in the opposite direction. No way were they going to face that massive beast!

MEET THE TOWER WIZARD

Red turned around and faced his ex-pets.

"You ran away," he said accusingly. "Did you not like me?"

Mindy gulped. "No, it's not that! It's just . . ."

"We have to get home!" Jack jumped in. "Our mother is worried about us."

"Oh." Red looked sad.

The twins were scared. What if Red forced them back into his cage? They were unsure what to think about the winged beast. Was he good or bad?

Suddenly Betty stepped forward. "Red, I want you to know that imprisoning people and animals is not good. You should let us be free."

"YOU CAN TALK?"

"But then I'll get lonely," whined Red.

The twins couldn't believe this humongous, powerful creature, with sharp pointy teeth and a wingspan that easily reached the size of their house, was acting like a baby!

"Well, we'll visit you!" offered Betty hopefully. "You just saved our lives. It's the least we can do in return."

"You'll visit?"

"Yeah!" said Mindy enthusiastically. "Even though this adventure has been very scary and life-threatening, it's the most fun I've ever had!"

Jack nodded. "Agreed."

Red seemed to ponder the idea for a few moments, then he nodded. "Okay. I'll let

MEET THE TOWER WIZARD

you go free. You are no longer my pets. Now, you are my friends!"

The twins and Betty cheered on while Dash pranced around barking madly.

"Okay, okay," laughed Jack. "Come on, let's go home now. We need to start walking to the portal."

"Do you want me to give you a ride?" asked Red.

"That would be awesome!" shouted Mindy.

They climbed upon his back and Red took off into the skies, heaving his wings and carrying their weight as if they were as light as a feather.

In the air, with the wind flowing through their hair and the peace of mind from

"YOU CAN TALK?"

knowing Red would protect them, the Nether looked quite beautiful with its glowing red stones and fiery lava lakes. Eventually Red began his decline and landed softly beside the Nether portal. They all got off and Betty leaned over and pecked Red on the cheek.

"Thank you!" said Betty gratefully.

Red blushed. It made his skin look even more red!

"It's nothing . . ." he mumbled.

Finally, the group of adventurers stood in front of the portal.

"Promise you'll visit?" called Red.

"We will!" replied Jack.

MEET THE TOWER WIZARD

They all nodded at each other and then the group jumped through the portal.

//

The Nether portal dumped them out like trash, and they fell in a heap together. They groaned at their aching bones, but suddenly Jack started laughing happily.

"We're alive!"

He kissed the cubic grass at their feet and laughed again. The others looked at him for a few seconds, and then they, too, joined him in laughter.

"Thank you, all of you," said Betty eventually. "In the end, I did need rescuing!"

They all hugged then turned to head back to the wizard's tower. Dash knew

"YOU CAN TALK?"

the way of course—he was such a smart dog! Before long they arrived at the giant wooden door. Mindy knocked three times, just like she did seemingly ages ago when they first arrived. There were some banging sounds and what sounded like a goat baying from behind the door. It took some time, but eventually the door swung open with a crash.

"Yes, who is it?" yelled Wizzler the Wizard, appearing with a crazy look in his eye. For some reason he had a toothbrush stuck in his beard.

"Wizzler!" said Jack apprehensively. "We're back! We rescued Betty!"

"Who are you people? I don't know you!"

At first the twins were devastated. If the wizard didn't know who they were, would

MEET THE TOWER WIZARD

he still help them get back home? Had they come all this way for nothing?

But then Betty stepped forward and bonked the wizard on the head with her hoof.

"Snap out of it, Wizzler," she snapped. "It's me, Betty. And you sent these kids to save me."

The wizard wiped his eyes and looked at them all again. Recognition alighted in his face.

"Ahh yes!" he shouted suddenly, startling the twins. "Of course, of course, I remember! Well done children, Dash, well done."

Betty rolled her eyes and pranced through the door. The wizard gestured for the twins and Dash to follow. Inside, it seemed like

"YOU CAN TALK?"

Wizzler was working on a kind of strange experiment. He had a weird glass disc on the table, with strange liquids and colors inside.

"What's this?" asked Jack curiously.

"Oh, just a new test of mine. I'm trying to make a new color."

"A new color?" exclaimed Jack.

"Yes. I'm trying to make a color that gives you the same feeling as when you bite into a really juicy apple."

"Oh, I see," said Jack, although he didn't really know what the wizard was saying.

"Well, it's nice to see you all," continued Wizzler. "But it's time you leave. I'm quite busy with this new experiment of mine."

MEET THE TOWER WIZARD

The twins' faces fell.

"Wizzler, you're forgetting something," scolded Betty.

"What am I forgetting?"

"The twins! You promised them you would help them get back home in return for saving me."

"Oh, yes! Right, well, that's easy. You could've done that on your own!"

"What do you mean?" asked Mindy in confusion.

"It's very simple,'' assured Wizzler. "Dash is a very special dog. If you hold onto his collar and he barks three times, then you will be transported right back home!"

"YOU CAN TALK?"

Jack's mouth fell open. "We could've gone back home long before this?"

Wizzler winced. "Oh, yeah. Sorry, I probably should've told you that in the first place."

"Why didn't you?" yelled Mindy, exasperated.

"Because I wanted Betty back!" complained Wizzler, suddenly seeming like a toddler. "I needed your help."

Mindy felt like pulling that white beard right off the wizard's face, but Betty stepped between them.

"Jack, Mindy, I know Wizzler can be . . . trying sometimes, but you have to trust me when I say he's a good person at heart. Really."

MEET THE TOWER WIZARD

The twins looked at Betty. They trusted her, and they had seen how brave and warmhearted she was. If she trusted Wizzler . . . Well, they supposed they could forgive him.

"How about I make it up to you?" said Wizzler excitedly.

"How?" the twins asked.

"Here." Wizzler snatched Betty's diamond helmet from her head.

"Hey!" she cried.

Wizzler winked at her then turned to the twins. "I can turn this diamond helmet into anything you'd like, and when you bring it back to your world it will keep its shape."

"Oh, I don't know if—" began Mindy, but Jack quickly interrupted her.

"We'd like a diamond cow figurine please!" he said.

Mindy remembered the cow figurine they had left in pieces back at home. She nodded enthusiastically.

"Ooh, yes please!" she cried.

The wizard smiled warmly then with a wave of his hands the helmet morphed into a figurine, exactly like the one they had destroyed back home!

"This is perfect! Our mother won't be mad now," said Mindy happily.

Suddenly Dash whined and stepped between the twins.

"Dash says it's time to go," said Wizzler.

MEET THE TOWER WIZARD

"Will we ever see you again?" asked Mindy.

"I'm sure you will!" comforted Betty. "After all, you can come here whenever you'd like as long as Dash is with you!"

"And maybe you can do some more tasks for me," suggested Wizzler. "I'll pay you, of course. Perhaps with some more diamonds?"

"I like the sound of that," said Jack, imagining a massive diamond bed. His friends would be so jealous!

Mindy and Jack placed their hands on Dash's collar. He barked once.

WOOF!

"If you're ever looking for adventure, you know where to go," said Betty.

"YOU CAN TALK?"

WOOF!

"Take care! Hopefully I'll still remember you next time you come," teased Wizzler.

And with Dash's great final **WOOF**, the world around them morphed and bent like water, and they were surrounded by sparkles. Then there was a big *woosh* and they were back in their living room, just as they had left it. The shattered remains of the old cow figurine laid at their feet.

"We're back!" gasped Mindy.

"Dash, you're a wonder!" cried Jack.

Dash barked again and hopped onto the couch, falling fast asleep. Mindy and Jack grinned but stopped as soon as they heard the sound of a car pulling into their driveway.

MEET THE TOWER WIZARD

"That's Mom!" said Mindy in a panic.

"Quick, let's clean this up before she sees!" Jack replied.

In lightning speed, they swept up the mess, placed the new diamond cow figurine the wizard gave them on the shelf, and sat on the couch with the TV on as if nothing had happened.

They heard footsteps and soon their mother stepped through the door with some grocery bags.

"Hi children," she called.

"Hi Mom!" they replied in unison.

Their mom glanced at the TV and tutted disapprovingly. "Have you been watching TV all day? It's not good for you; it'll

"YOU CAN TALK?"

turn your eyes into boxes! You should go outside, find an adventure!"

As she walked off into the kitchen, Mindy and Jack took one look at each other and burst out laughing.

Dash groaned and tried to cover his ears with his paws, but their laughter was too loud.

"She's right, we need to use our imaginations, like we do when we play Minecraft," agreed Mindy, momentarily catching her breath before the twins peeled into yet another round of laughter and headed into the yard.

Read the series in any order!

Book 1   Book 2   Book 3

Book 4   Book 5   Book 6

Join Rick Redstone's mailing list at
rickredstone.com

MEET THE AUTHOR

Rick Redstone is not just obsessed with writing. He's obsessed with Minecraft, and has been playing since the early days of the game.

A professional writer, Rick now channels his knowledge of Minecraft into

MEET THE TOWER WIZARD

adventure-packed chapter books for early readers.

Rick quickly saw how his nephew, Jasper, a reluctant reader, started embracing books once he got his hand on a few great Minecraft adventures. He has been inspired to keep writing to help other kids experience the same love of reading, so his books feature plenty of builds and lots of action to keep Minecraft fans' interest up.

Keep an eye on Rick's profile for more books soon - he is just warming up!

Made in the USA
Middletown, DE
18 August 2023

36814986R00076